Soo
Endogo book 6

Published by Crossbridge Books
Worcester
© Crossbridge Books 2025

ISBN 978-1-916945-15-9

British Library Cataloguing Publication Data. A catalogue record for this book is available from the British Library.

CROSSBRIDGE
BOOKS

Soo

Endogo book 6

by R M Price-Mohr

Vocabulary for book 6:

an
beach
came
chased
could
crab
day
find
I
keep
old
one/One
said
shells
so
Soo
we/We
went
were
you

Foreword for teachers

These books have been developed for older beginner readers. The research-based approach focuses on the recognition of just 100 key words that together make up approximately two-thirds of all reading matter in English. By the time the reader has learnt to recognise all the words in book 6, they will know 36 words that make up 33% of all reading matter in English written narrative.

For each new book, twenty new words are introduced and listed at the beginning of each book The new vocabulary for each book should be introduced to the learner in such a way that they will be able to recognise them at sight <u>before</u> reading the book. It is recommended that this is achieved through playing with the printed words. In the first instance, this should be by having two sets of printed and separated words in large font (minimum 20 point) that the beginner reader can match. It is crucial that the teacher continuously verbalise the words, and they may point to significant features in words, firstly the initial letters and secondly to any other distinctive features, to assist with the matching. Following this, the word recognition can be reinforced in games such as bingo, dominoes, snap, Pelmanism etc.

Some temptations to continue to avoid:

- Do not ask the reader to sound out all the individual letters of a word – only the initial letter has value at this stage for reading.
- Do not test the reader to see if they can recognise any of the words by telling you what they say – this should become obvious during the games; remember that visual recognition is not the same thing as verbalising what is seen.

This is Soo the endogo.

One day, Soo was looking for Max in the rain forest.

She could not find him in the forest.

So she went to the beach.

Max and Omo were on the beach looking for shells.

They want some shells to keep their food in.

"I was looking for you," said Soo.

"We are looking for shells," said Omo.

Soo went to look for shells on the beach too.

She found an old crab shell.

Max and Omo came to have a look too.

Suddenly, a very big crab came up the beach.

The crab chased Soo, Max, and Omo up the beach.

High Frequency Words:

an
came
could
day
find
I
keep
old
one
said
so
went
we
you

Word Patterns:

_ee_	see
	seen
	green
	tree
	keep
_oo	Soo
	too

www.ingramcontent.com/pod-product-compliance
Lightning Source LLC
LaVergne TN
LVHW010316070426

835510LV00024B/3402